Dedicated to:

Zoe McCurdy and Lizette Wachtel my soul sisters.

All the women and girls who are still living their trauma, you are loved, you are not alone, when the time is right for you, take that first step towards healing, there is hope.

And not forgetting Rob and Sammy two very special horses.

For Every Abused Girl and Woman, There Is Hope

A Pocket Full Of Seaglass is a book I originally wanted to be about my weight loss journey, people who know me and who have seen my massive transformation over the course of 18 months, had been asking how I did it, how did I lose so much weight and get so fit.

But when I began writing I realised there was so much more involved than just losing weight, so decided to include my whole story, I have tried to write about my childhood trauma for a number of years but only now felt I was in the right space to make a real attempt.

Like Seaglass I have transformed from broken into something beautiful.

If you are looking for a well written organised book, you are definitely in the wrong place, healing from trauma is not organised or pretty.

I could have gone back and rewritten everything into a nice tidy ordered book, but that wouldn't be true to myself, this is how I wrote it, how buried memories came up as I was writing my story for the first time.

I feel it does show the reality of surviving childhood trauma, from the happy feel of chapter 1 to the near breakdown during the writing of chapter 3.

I hope my story will help anyone who has experienced trauma like and who are still out there hiding their trauma not living a life they deserve, I know there are many of you, you are not alone, you are enough , you deserve every happiness,

you are loved, one day you will believe this, if this is you, please seek professional help, a google search will direct you to local services who can help or speak to your Doctor.

This is not a self help book, or a quick fix weight loss book, just the story of an ordinary woman who hopes to inspire others.

Each song chosen for each chapter is a song that has a special meaning for me and helped me on my journey.

A Pocket Full Of Sea Glass

A Journey of Weight Loss and Healing

Chapter 1

Leaving on a Jet Plane – John Denver

To answer the question I get all the time, "How did you end up here"?

Heathrow Airport

Well this is it, Terminal 2 The Queens Terminal, OK I'm still crying as I did all the way from Oxfordshire to Heathrow, I've said my goodbyes to my kids at the coach station, I cried so much I could hardly say where I was going, I don't know what the coach driver thought and as for the rest of the coach, well they were just staring, who can blame them a 49 year old woman totally losing it.

This is my Shirley Valentine/Midlife Crisis depending on your view, you see I was a teaching assistant with 3 kids grown up but still at home, mortgage, living in Oxfordshire for 22 years, until I had this great idea to get a pen pal on death row in America, I'm a kind caring type person, did a lot of courses in psychology which I thought would be useful, I also have a weird thing where I want to save everybody, I suppose that's not a bad thing but even I can't save anyone from death row, but I could spread a little happiness, by sending letters of hope, for fucks sake that sounds so happy clappy but that's how I was a total do gooder.

Anyway my kids were not up for their mum no matter how crazy I am to be writing to someone on death row, they had visions of relatives or murders knocking on the door, so that was out of the question.

Plan B joined an online pen pal site, well you can imagine the amount of weirdos I had to wade through before I found someone nice and normal, he's from Cork Ireland and yes we did fall in love, thanks to WhatsApp and video calls, I did fly out to meet him one Valentine's day for the first time, me being scared of flying still made it to Cork Airport complete with Valentine's card and a box of chocolates.

I came thorough the doors scared as hell feeling like a teenager on a first date, trying to breathe in so hard I was almost going blue, I haven't quite mentioned I'm fat, I was hoping with my newly done hair he wouldn't notice the fat, I pushed my boobs out further to make them bigger than my stomach. He was smaller than I thought having told me he was 5ft 10 I'm 5ft 7 and he's shorter than me, that was the first thing I said, while I was hugging him to death you're not 5ft 10, not the most romantic thing to say, we laughed he had only said that because he thought it sounded better the 5ft 5, men can be so strange, little did I know Irish men are a total different breed. Wow the smell of him and just being able to touch him and kiss him was the most wonderful feeling, I bloody hope he felt the same, we had 3 nights together whatever.

He never mentioned my fatness although I know he noticed, he was kind enough not to say anything, the nicknames came later, Snuffleupagus the elephant from Sesame Street now that really hurt, he was joking apparently and big foot, I'll explain that later.

After a number of visits, and the way the locals made me so welcome from day one, we decided I should make Cork my home, as in myself and my boyfriend not the locals deciding I should make Cork my home.

I must mention the Cork accent, it's not the easiest to understand and my first few trips were spent saying sorry I didn't catch that, they can speak quite quickly and what the hell is a press? Was told to put the shopping in the press, I thought what the hell I'll put it in the cupboard, lucky that's the same thing, there's a hot press which is the airing cupboard kinda figured that for myself, didn't want to look totally like a dumb blonde.

Dumb I'm not, blonde I am, even though it's topped up from a bottle, I still get blonde moments even when my dark roots are showing.

This how I ended up at Heathrow airport on a hot May day in 2017, wearing a the worst blouse I could find, bright red with blue flowers, what possessed me I hate flowery clothes, with the song Final Countdown running through my head, this is it I'm leaving England for good, house sold, kids grown up and living together, left my job and I'm on my way.

Just carrying a large handbag, hope they don't look though it, my knickers are in there along with other stuff I couldn't fit into my small hand luggage bag, it's a nice red colour but only fitted the essential clothes, a Nirvana CD and The Bridges of Madison County book.

See what I mean travelling to my new life like a hippie with no possessions, I guess you could be forgiven for thinking I'm having a midlife crisis but I'm in love and willing to do whatever it takes for us to be together.

My flight is delayed, end up sitting with an old Irish lady, who gave me advice on living with an Irish man, they can be controlling, don't let him boss you around, they like their own way, they are set in their ways and won't change for anything, hell this isn't helping, anyway I'm sure my man is nothing like that, they do say it as it is not fluffing things up something I had better get used to.

Gates open now, we can board, I hope I'm not sitting near the old lady, I don't think I could take an hour of her advice, it's ok it's an Asian man, I've got a window seat, I want to see Ireland as I arrive, but first I see London slipping away, I wonder how long it will be before I see it again. Oh no his snoring not just snoring but facing me and snoring who does that, I'm staring at him willing him to wake up and oh no his eyes open and he's looking right at me, I quickly fumble in my bag for a sweet, he doesn't sleep for the rest of the flight, guess I freaked him out, probably thought I was a 50 year old psycho.

I can see the sea it's beautiful with the sun shining on it, that's Cork just coming into view, I start crying, it's the start of my new life, I'm happy and sad all at the same time.

Landing is perfect it's 9.30pm the latest I've ever flown, warm here same as over, I carry my jacket, right straight to the toilets must touch up my make up I don't want to arrive at my new home looking like a troll.

It's a strange feeling I'm all alone at Cork airport, with all my possessions, he's not here to meet me I said it's not worth spending money on a taxi both ways, he can't drive, I wish he was here I really do feel all alone, I've left everything behind, my kids, my job, my home, I feel kind of lost.

I stand for awhile watching people finding their loved ones, dashing off for buses and taxis, heading home, I envy them, they live here, they are settled, it's still new to me, I feel so English, I hope I can be successful here and make a good life for both of us.

Better find a taxi, I've been told to haggle the price and not go on the meter, he's from Nigeria we agree on 50 euros and I'm on my way to a little village in Cork., so nervous I talking none stop, taxi driver must think I'm on speed, I'm recognising places we pass, the big lake, nearly there now.

I'm hot and tired but excited, this is what I've dreamed of for so long and now it's happening, we turn into the village, it all looks the same, there's the pub, lovely place, great landlord, spent many a happy night there, the local people are so friendly they really made it easier to move here, I feel so accepted by them, I wasn't even sure at first if they would like me but they do even though I'm English and the whole history we have of starving, killing, and generally being total bastards to the Irish people, look up Black and Tans, what they did was horrific, they have every right to hate me but they don't.

I've arrived, panic over he's outside the door waiting for me, my phone doesn't work here so been out of contact since I left the airport, OMG I'm here I've done it, can't wait to get out of this taxi, but I'm so excited I'm fumbling for the cash then decided to tip him because he had to put up with my insane ramblings all the way from Cork Airport.

Girls Just Want to Have Fun – Cyndi Lauper

Look at the Cut of Ya

I finally get out of the taxi and run into his arms, hugging each other so hard, Welcome home, the best words I've ever heard, I'm so tired and emotional, we dump my bag in our bedroom, "what the fuck are you wearing", he's noticed my hideous blouse, it's bright red with big blue flowers, resembling curtains from the 70s era, oh dear I've been hating it all day, I put my leather jacket on just to cover it and we head for the local pub.
Vodka and lemonade is much needed, I'm tired but happy, we walk in the pub and it's like I've never been away, we find a table in a quiet corner, it's romantic and he leans towards me and says you look like someone out of Def Leppard, yeah I'll give him that, the black leather and big blonde hair, I think I'm looking good but he's just said I look like a man, oh dear I'm not the hot blonde I thought I was, probably because I'm 49, fat and not hot at all although I can look good in my Facebook profile, due to airbrushing and camera angles.
The locals we know say welcome home, it feels so good that I'm accepted here, it's the start of a new era for both of us.
I'm not sure he knows what he's let himself in for living with me, he's never lived with a woman for any length of time and now here I was going to be a permanent fixture in his life.

Now the fun starts, I'm here for good, sharing a bungalow with my partner and his younger brother and a yellow lab called Babe, all good so far, I'm scared his brother doesn't like me, of course we've met a few times but I'm worried he'll be thinking I will want to take over which I wouldn't want to do anyway.

And Babe had a look in her eye as if to stay is that bitch really staying.

Although they live together they have very separate lives each doing their own thing, which was fine but with me in the mix I'm hoping it doesn't cause problems.

Massive problem for me when can I safely go to the toilet when no one can hear me, OK I've got toilet issues, it's ok to go in the pub I can watch and make sure they are empty, yep weird middle age woman watching the toilets is totally normal, well it is for me.

I'll worry about that later, for the moment we are enjoying each other's company and the alcohol which by the way I'm not a massive drinker due to having to get up for work all my life, however I'm pretty sure I'll get used to drinking.

Well that was what I told everyone, I'm not a big drinker but that wasn't entirely true.

Four vodka and 7ups later and I'm getting tired, he's had a few pints we're going home, yes home to our bed, that makes it feel more secure, I'm hoping this is going to work out and he won't get bored of me, I'm kind of fucked if he does, homeless and jobless in a new country scares the hell out of me, I'm going to stay positive after all I love him to bits.

We head for home, a 2 minute walk and hell that walk up the drive feels really long after a few drinks, back to our bedroom, it's not massive and with the double bed in it, it's even smaller, my side is a bloody nightmare I have to crawl up the bed from the bottom because it's right up against the wall, not great when I'm trying to be sexy, ended up looking like a something from a horror film crawling up the bed all messy hair wearing a t-shirt, why oh why can't I ever manage to look sexy.

Also I there's no bedside lamp on my side of the bed so there's a lot of crawling around in the dark and it is so dark here, coming from a city where it's never really dark, this is going to take a bit of getting used to, I don't actually like the dark, always had the landing light on or even my bedroom light sometimes, I didn't know people slept in total darkness.

I'm hoping his brother will never see me walking crablike along the wall until I feel the bathroom light switch, he would be scarred for life and probably need therapy.

Ok here's the curve ball, three years ago I had a massive mental breakdown, suicidal, had urges to jump off tall buildings, apparently the meds I had been given made things worse until they settled, it's fine said the doctor when I phoned to say I felt like jumping of buildings, just keep taking the tablets it's will pass, oh and I was also told the tablets are not addictive, wrong, so very wrong, yes I was a prescription junkie, I could the doctor to give me anything and always upped the dose until I reached the max, then would get prescribed the stronger stuff, I was a walking zombie for ages, spent 6 weeks spaced out on my sofa once when they prescribed me antipsychotics by mistake, my kids made me toast and tea while the doctors kept saying double the dose every other day, I was happy sleeping and talking to dead people.

It took a trip to A & E when I couldn't walk or talk anymore, well I could talk but it came out scrambled and I could crawl, anyway the doctor took one look at the pills and said throw them away, you should never have been given them, of course I didn't throw them away, I was so addicted to them, eventually came off them and weirdly walked up Snowdon the week after, I felt so alive.

I've been off meds for just 6 months, I'm hoping I can cope without them, I also get panic attacks and have PTSD, so making this move has been much more of a challenge as far as my mental health goes, I'm very keen to appear normal although my children agree I couldn't be normal for long, I always end up doing something a little bit weird, hell I'm a mother who lost her 19 year old daughter in a clothes shop and found her sitting by a display only it wasn't her, it was a shop dummy, well it did look like her from a distance, anyway incidents like that kind of confirmed to my children that I was crazy but in a good way.

Here I am the adventure begins, I'm more positive and happy than I've been in a long time, I was on anti depressants until November last year, if anyone ever tells you that talking about things will be a weight off your shoulders don't believe them, I learnt the hard way, I finally disclosed to the police the sexual abuse I went through as a 14 year old, he was an older man who successfully groomed me and my parents who allowed him to take me to London his home town for weekends, the police investigated my friend gave a statement, my mum gave a statement but my friend from back then who I had been friends with for 32 years refused to give a statement saying it would be mud slinging and the perpetrator was a friend of her brother, she was also very rude to the investigating officer who had by this time found and arrested him the other end of the country, more on this in chapter 3.

To cut a long story short it never made it to court due to lack of evidence and my friend of 32 years is no longer my friend, sometimes it's better to walk away.

So leaving all that behind is refreshing and although I'm still having nightmares now and again I seem to be doing well without the meds.

Although the woman who works in our local pub has managed to trigger me very badly after she approached me from behind and whispered in my ear "Stella, can you both stay to help lock up", OK she didn't know my history but hell I was a mess for days, then got all angry because these days people should respect personal space of others and as for whispering in someone's ear please don't.

On a more cheerful note I have managed to get myself stuck in a pub door, with one arm across me trying not to squash a roll up, must lose weight fast these doorways are not made for my fat arse.

Chapter 3 I Remember Everything – Five Finger Death Punch

A Daughter of a Narcissistic Mother

To understand the present we must first understand the past (this must be a stolen quote I read somewhere, no idea where but I like it)

It has taken me years to even begin to make sense of my childhood.

Narcissism wasn't something I had heard of when I was growing up, so my references to it now are from what I learned later in life and she fits the profile, at the time I just thought my mother had a mental illness along with being a closet lesbian. I unfortunately wasn't the Golden Child, that was my younger sister Julie, there is only us two so guess I got the short straw, well that's how I used to think but looking back now I see how this made me the strong woman I am today, hell I'm sounding like a positive meme.

My earliest memories of childhood are not of a happy family, laughter, fun and all the ups and downs of a happy childhood.

The earliest memories I have are of fear and pain, being thrown across belly first across Lego on the floor because I didn't want to pick it up, having my urine soaked pants wiped in my face because I wet myself again, I learned early on not to show love for anything.

I had a favourite toy lamb which I dropped into some ice cream on the street while shopping with my mum, most mothers would take it home and wash it, but not mine she made me throw it in the bin, I didn't want to and I'm sure the whole High Street was watching as she made me throw my favourite toy away, I learned not to cry , don't give her the satisfaction, she was brutal, hitting me a lot, my bottom was covered in red raised hand prints, she never marked my face
.

I also often woke up to her pulling my bed covers up, she always said my covers were falling off, which was not the case, my bed was tucked in tight, It was years later when I had my own children, I I realised that that behaviour wasn't normal, my kids never kicked their covers off on a nightly basis, along with mums words to me before I went to sleep one night "I can do anything to you while you are asleep and you wouldn't know anything about it" I was about 7 years old when she said that, I was sleeping with a lamp on for over 50 years because of that.

I went to counselling as an adult and what ever mum was doing to me while I was asleep, I wasn't ready to unblock it, let's just leave it there.

Happily we lived 4 doors away from grandparents , my dads parents who doted on my I was their favourite grandchild and mum hated it, believing it should be my sister as she was the one who looked like my mums side of the family, dark haired and large nose, I was like my dad's family blonde hair, blue eyes and tall.

Unfortunately mum couldn't have me happy so we had to move near her parents so she could look after them, they were elderly and not in good health, so we moved 4 miles away from my grandparents who adored me and gave me a safe place go to, also my friends who lived in the same street, I was 7 and about to start Brownies with my best friend.

My mum's parents moved away within the year, which goes to show, they couldn't get away from her quick enough.
It was a small village, my parents didn't drive so we were completely cut off, I couldn't attend any after school clubs or any discos or hang out with friends after school, there were a few kids in the village we were all different ages but we all used to hang around together, swimming in the river, building camps, the usual stuff.

I was terrified starting a new primary school, I had friends at my old house and was about to start Brownies with my best friend, looking back I totally understand why mum made us move, she was about to lose control of me, I was just going to start going out into the world and socializing with others, where I might discover how dysfunctional my family was, it's a typical narcissistic thing to do in order to keep control.

I refused to speak for a while at school in case I said the wrong thing and mum found out, I was happy to be known as very shy, it saved people digging any deeper.

So I was the quiet shy girl who didn't break the rule and kept her head down out of trouble at all times because they trouble at home would be far worse than any trouble at school.
There was worse to come, the school bus trip, it was a double decker bus, primary kids had to sit downstairs and secondary kids upstairs, I was fine until I went to secondary school.

Sitting up stairs on the bus with all the big kids was awful, the smokers sat at the back and the weird ones at the front, I usually sat somewhere in the middle, with my friend who lived up the road from me, she was a year above me at school, unfortunately due to her studies she wasn't always on the bus in the afternoon, and that's when one of the older boys targeted me for some special attention, he would come and sit next to me with his arm around me and talk about sex and draw pictures in the seam on the windows, while everyone laughed.

I was mortified but was too scared to tell anyone, I even missed the bus a couple of times on purpose to avoid him, a teacher taking me home asked too many questions so couldn't do that again.

We had no phone at home because, mum said it wasn't worth putting one in as we were going to be moving, 10 years later we moved, mum didn't want me to be able to phone for help.
I had a doctor in the town we moved from so I didn't go to the doctor as it was a taxi ride away, I was not registered at a dentist although I asked to be, she said the school dentist is enough and refused.

You see I was kept away from anyone who might ask questions.

Many years later an aunt who collected my parents and me as a baby from the hospital told me she had said I had the long fingers of dads family and mum was furious.
I must have sensed it, apparently I would never take a full bottle and was always being taking to the doctor for not eating.

In my teenage years she would hold my nose and force feed me which would result in me screaming and the neighbour running round to see what was happening, and instead of reporting her they actually assisted her in covering up the abuse, when it was thought she had broken my fingers as I tried to defend myself as a teenager, my neighbours helped us make up a story for the hospital and school, both of which were suspicious.

My English teacher actually kept me behind after class, I wrote a whole essay on abuse and based it on my life, he asked me if it was a true story, I said no I made it up, it's not real, got excellent marks for it but he was highly suspicious, I knew he didn't believe me but in those days there was nothing else he could do.

Do I wish I had spoken up then, yes I do but I was so trained in secrecy there was no way I could and if things went wrong I really thought my mum would kill me.

Mum's behaviour towards me got much worse as I grew up, developing into a young woman and needing privacy, whenever we moved house the first thing mum did was to remove the lock from the bathroom door "incase anyone got ill in the bath, they could drown" which is a total load of bollocks, sorry but writing this is making me so angry, I'm stopping for a coffee to calm down, it's so hard to write this chapter, feeling those feelings again never gets any easier, let's all stop for a coffee, I recommend Kenco Cappuccino sachets unsweetened.

I'm back refreshed and calm, thanks to the healing power of a Cappuccino, back to mum and the bathroom door, this was all part of mums control, having no lock on the bathroom made life very difficult, as a teenage girl I didn't want anyone seeing my body, but every time I had a bath mum would "need something from the bathroom" and come in, I would cover myself with a towel, but it got so often, I started to roll a towel up and stuff it against the door so she couldn't get in, I was sure she was a lesbian, always looking at my body, by the time I was 14 mum was buying me stockings and suspenders and make up, I have a photo of me aged 15 looking like a little hooker, with my hair up in a French pleat and a face fully made up, I feel sick just looking at it.

I attended a 70th wedding anniversary party in the village hall that night, everyone was there and some strangers, an old man kept asking for a kiss and I refused, my friend said let him he's just an old man, it will make him happy I turned my check so he could kiss my check and he grabbed by face turned it towards him and stuck his tongue down my throat I was totally humiliated, this was in the middle of the room, not a quiet corner, my friend, him and his friend laughed and laughed I got the house key of mum and went home.

My mum would not have done anything even if I had told her, I know she knew what happened anyway, she would have loved that I was upset.

I haven't mentioned my dad, he lived with us but liked a quiet life away from the drama of my mum, so he spent all his time at work never taking days off, never having a sick day, if he wasn't at work he was growing vegetables, he either didn't know or closed his eyes to what mum was doing to me, it was just me, I spoke to my sister, one of the few occasions we did speak and she had a totally different life to me as she was mums little lamb as she was called.

Mum and dad never hugged me, I do remember my sister sitting with mum all hugs and kisses, I never wanted to be touched by anyone, when I gave birth to my first child dad shook my hand and said well done, the nurses faces were a picture.

When I was 14 years old a man in his twenties from London started lodging in the village , he had a car and soon became friends with all the teenagers, which looking back now was weird, I was the ideal victim being quiet and having a bad time at home, he lodged next door to my friend had easy access to information, at the time I enjoyed the attention from someone who was nice to me, I was very shy and quiet and he was able to gain my trust and bought mum flowers and chocolates, talked to my dad and they let him take me to London at weekends, how the hell they thought that was ok, I would never have let my daughters get into a situation like that.

Let me describe myself at 14, I was a very young 14, skinny, no boobs, tom boyish by with longish blonde hair and blue eyes, never had a boyfriend and was being physically abused at home, the perfect target for grooming , it wasn't difficult to groom me and my parents, although I am convinced my mum knew what was going on and allowed it because it would hurt me, it is common for nassisstic mothers to allow their daughters to be abused by older men.

I thought it was love, because I had no idea what love was.
I was easily impressed by a Ford Cortina and a London address.
I was taken to Wimpy, I had never seen a Wimpy Burger Bar before and Steakhouse I felt so out of my depth eating out, my family never ate out anywhere.

Clubs and pubs were so busy and I felt so young, I was young, but was made up to look older when out, I did get scared when he spotted some guys he had been to school with and we had to make a quick get away, he said they were trouble but thinking about it now, he didn't want them to see him with a 14 year old.

I even thought having cheese and wine was classy, no it wasn't, it was to get me drunk, so stupid but in my mind that was better than life at home.

He was very clever about evidence, he made sure I washed myself and my clothes, at the time he said he was a clean freak and it was healthy to be clean etc....
I now know it was to get rid of any trace of evidence.
He trained me to give pleasure to him sexually and yes it was really training, and he could be very nasty if I didn't do as I was told, of course this left me unable to understand real relationships and thought sex was just providing for the other person and if they didn't want it, they didn't love me.
Never felt good enough, was always trying be good enough for him for my mum, never made the grade or if I did no one told me, years later and I'm a total people pleaser.

I was too young and vulnerable to understand this was toxic and controlling, I was just a kid who craved love and affection, but had no idea what it really was.
One weekend I was there and his friend and girlfriend came to visit, when I was left alone with the girlfriend she asked how old I was, I told her 14 and she looked visibly shocked, she said I was too young and it wasn't right what he was doing and I should get out as soon as possible.

I wish I knew who she was, to thank her, in all the years of abuse she was the only one who said anything.

But without going into details I didn't get away from him until 6 months later, it didn't matter, the damage was done years before by my mum, this just added to the trauma.

I found a large envelope of letters in his room, yes I was snooping, I sensed something was wrong, it was full of letters from girls as young as I was who he had had relationships with over years, he collected virgins.
I understood why he made me write to him one time and give him a photo.

Mum's comment when she found out he wasn't taking me to London anymore "ha I knew nobody is going to want you, you are good for nothing"

Mum spent a lot of time making sure I would never feel good enough, job well done, I still don't ever feel good enough, no matter what I achieve in life.

He moved on to his next virgin he only wanted virgins he was counting up how many he could have, she didn't last long with him and sadly took an overdose after he dumped her, she survived thankfully.

I feel I'm spewing this out quickly, not going into as much detail as I could, because I don't want this book to be about my past, I could write a whole book about it, maybe I will one day.
There were a few people who I know for sure knew what my mum was doing to me and didn't take that step and report her and the man from London, as far as I'm concerned they are as guilty as her for keeping quiet.

Anyway to cut along chapter short, I came out of my childhood and teenage years, abused, broken, traumatised, with PTSD, Depression, Panic Attacks, self harming and an addiction to prescription medication, not to mention the years of numbing the pain with alcohol and illegal drugs.
A Heroin addict saved my life, we started dating in the late 80s, I was 19 at the start, I didn't know he was a heroin addict until he shot up in front of me during our first date, at his bedsit, the look of shock on my face, he said I thought you knew, like it was common knowledge.

I have to add I was stoned at his brother's house with a couple of friends when we first met so he must have just thought I knew all about him.

 I had no idea but said it's not a problem, only I could even think Heroin addiction is not a problem, hey just go ahead I'm fine with it, unbelievable thinking but he was a lovely person and anyone who wasn't going to abuse me in anyway was a good person.

We were both troubled and damaged souls.
I never gave him money but bought him food, paid electricity etc.
I was a high functioning drug user, I was able to work full time.

Never bought or sold drugs, never had a criminal record, people just gave me stuff, drugs and alcohol.
We smoked weed all the time which was great for me and took speed which was also great but he would never let me do heroin, I really wanted to, I wanted to be numb from the pain of my past but he said no, it's highly addictive and he didn't want me going down the same road he was, robbing places to feed his addiction, prison time again and again.

I respected his judgement and never took heroin, although I can make a great tea from Opium Poppies, please do not try this, it is highly illegal, have him to thank for saving my life, I would have taken it and it would probably have killed me, maybe he could see that in me, sadly he passed away a few years ago, I did get a phone call telling me he had passed although we had not been in contact for over 20 years, we split up because basically we were 2 broken people and it wasn't helping either of us, so I left, it broke my heart but I had to save myself.

Life with a Heroin addict is stressful, along with prison visits, him being on the run, bedsits where you can't open the door if there is a knock, well I couldn't when I was alone, he could of course, the look what I bought conversation as he showed me a gun, I was so scared it would go off by mistake, only for protection.

I think when I was approached by a plain clothes detective in Thames Valley Police CID, asking if I would be willing to be wired up and go to London on the next drugs run with my boyfriend to allow them to get evidence against a Mr Big, I started to open my eyes to how deep I was in.
The detective had it all planned, how they would listen and then force their way in and arrest everyone, including me so as not to get anyone suspicious, but I would be released afterwards.

No way would I be involved in anything like that, I had chosen my side years ago and it wasn't with the police, I turn him down and he had a long chat with me about what I was involved with and the dangers.

To be fair it did hit home and it did scare me, I wasn't a tough streetwise girl, but I enjoyed the protection I had from my boyfriend and his friends, nobody would touch me or my family or property because of who he was and his reputation and there was always someone to look after me when he was in prison.

I was looked after and loved, that's all I ever wanted, to feel safe and protected, in my twisted way of thinking this was perfect, but the reality of it was far from perfect.

The holes in the wall from him hitting with a hammer when he was coming down, the nightmares where I slept on the floor at the bottom of the bed for my own safety, thought he might kill me in my sleep he was fighting his nightmares. I came out of that relationship with more issues added to those I already had, when I first started seeing him, I found out that my medical records had been checked, I was told by his friend they had someone in a hospital who checked, which made all the strange questions at the beginning make sense, like have you ever been in hospital? I thought it was just chat, but they were checking I was telling the truth, which I did, appendix out at 13 and miscarriage at 17, apparently this is normal for checking the trust of a person, they are very careful who gets close.

For years after I was scared to see a doctor because I didn't think my notes were secure.
I was lucky to come out of this without a criminal record. He is the reason I went into schools educating children about drugs, I had to save someone, I couldn't save him so I tried to save everyone else
.

Addiction is an illness and sadly not everyone can be saved, some of the best people I have known were addicts and cared for me much more than my own family.

Along with the Domestic Violence education for women, and a helpline, I was out to save everyone but me.

Had to leave that project as it was getting harder and harder to cover up that I was really a domestic violence survivor, I never talked about, people thought I was just doing a really good job helping women understand domestic violence and where to get help, they had no idea I was living in a domestic violence relationship while setting up the project, beyond crazy but it seemed a perfectly sane thing to do at the time. I left the project and did eventually leave the relationship. I got a stalker, honestly I haven't made this up, my life has really been this messed up, I started going to church, and met some lovely friendly people, one day while shopping a man said hello I recognise you from church, I didn't know him but said hello and wham that was the beginning of an hellish time, he would be everywhere, on my route to school everyday, inviting me to his house, just following me around , if I wasn't there he would ask my friend where I was, I even started hiding behind cars to avoid him, I didn't report him as there was no stalking law at the time and I didn't think the police would do anything, he did start getting nasty because I was avoiding him but suddenly he died, alcohol was involved I think, I know he was having appointments at the local mental health hospital. All this had made me scared and paranoid, I was not a strong person.

During this time I began drinking to feel better, it doesn't work, you feel worse and drink more to feel better and it's a vicious cycle. I had a friend with similar issues who became my drinking partner, we were both on meds and alcohol, trying to drown out our lives.

I was blonde haired, she was brown haired, we were a down market Edie and Patsy from Ab Fab, my children were the opposite of me, they were quiet had friends but didn't like night clubs or drinking and smoking, it was me coming home at 3am carrying my glittery stilettos waking my daughter because I'm locked out and pissed.

Didn't stop nightclubbing until I was 45, we often had dreams of living in a nightclub, or cocktail bar, could we buy our favourite table and just live there.
My daughter had to pick us up in her car on a few occasions pissed out of heads and unable to get home, this I'm not proud of but it happened.

One of these occasions was a trip to the park with bottles of wine in brown paper bags and loads of cigarettes, we spent the day on the bandstand, sitting, then laying then just so pissed we couldn't walk straight, my daughter collected us, we finally found our way out of the park, I then went to look at my friends shed roof for no apparent reason.
The next day we would text each other and compare symptoms, we were both on meds which shouldn't be mixed with alcohol.
We are no longer in contact, we were very close, like sisters and me moving to Cork was hard for her and basically I just left, no goodbye I just went, I needed a fresh start and she was part of my past now.

I know that sounds hard but I did it for me we were co-dependent on each other, yes we kept each other sane to a certain extent but the drinking was way out of control.
My work life was also affected, I was on a course when the woman tutor came up behind me and run her fingers through my pony tail, saying I wish I had hair like you, I just froze, flash backs of my mum's weird behaviour and the sexual abuse flying through my head so fast, my head was spinning, I felt physically sick and was when I arrived home.

I did write an official complaint against the tutor, for which I received an apology, my manager was very good about it and counselling was offered but I refused, I still wasn't ready, although I knew I wasn't handling life very well, I could feel the stress building even then.

Should I have got help then, probably, with hindsight yes I should have but at the time I did what I felt was right for me, I didn't want the pain of counselling, it hurts to talk about it. Buried it again, but for how long?

Things were not going to change unless I did something to confront my past, it wasn't going away, and I wasn't coping. I finally got the strength to report the man from London at the age of 50, thanks to the Jimmy Savile case, it drove me crazy all the reports daily in the news, I was drinking more and more and getting angry that people were talking about historical sexual abuse, I just wanted them to shut up and stop reminding me, in the end I phoned the local police station and made an appointment to meet with a Sargent from the historic sexual abuse department, I made a statement which was typed up.
I returned to read and sign it, she promised she would find him and she did, she phoned me a month later, she had found him and met him and his lawyer at his local police station which was the other end of the country.

Unfortunately happy endings only happen in fairy tales, the Crown Prosecution Service in England refused to go to Court due to lack of evidence, some witnesses had died (his parents) and my friend of 37 years refused to give a statement due to him being a friend of her brother and it would be just mud slinging, she is no longer my friend.

By then I had no fight left in me, I thought by telling the police a weight would be lifted off my shoulders and everything would be fine, it wasn't they don't tell you life gets a whole lot worse, worse than you can even imagine, I ended up having a complete breakdown, self harming, suicidal and was just hurting so much, this happened soon after I gave the statement, I remember going into work in a complete daze like I was outside my body, my manager asked if I was OK, and when I spoke I didn't recognize my own voice it was kind of a slowed down version of me, I was sent home and ended up on sick leave for months, my doctor prescribed antidepressants, these made me want to jump off tall buildings, I had to be watched for 2 weeks until the pills settled in my system, then things got worse, I was taking more and more, just to get me through the day, my doctor said I could double the dose every other day, which I gladly did and became a zombie basically, my kids had to go through this with me, looking after me and themselves, they were working adults by then so at least they were not tiny children, they were fantastic in a very difficult time, difficult time, it was hell on earth, I don't know why I'm trying to down play it.

I remember managing to get my doctor to prescribe the real deal, not a synthetic version of my meds a very controlled and difficult to get extra strong version, which I got, it said take one 10mg tablet a day, no way was that going to work, I was already on over 40mg a day so I took 4, just finished taking them when my doctor phoned to say only take one they are very strong, that's fine I said to her, thinking shit I've taken 4 already, totally zombiefied for the night and next day but I liked it that way, comfortably numb as Pink Floyd would say.

I did cold turkey to get off the meds not long before I moved to Ireland, it was a bit of risk as to weather I could manage without them but here I am 3 years later and still off them, I feel like I'm kind of sugar coating this a bit, cold turkey was hell, stomach pains, everything sounded loud, loads of sleep or no sleep, I was also talking to dead people and Jehovah witnesses who called to the house, no idea what I said to them but the became regular callers with their magazine, the Jehovah's witnesses that is not the dead people.

The reality of trauma is it never really goes away, it's taken me 6 months to write this chapter as I didn't really want to go there, my brain has started blocking things again, I'm forgetting basic things like my cash card number, times I have to be at places, I'm asking again and again but keep forgetting, it's my brains way of keeping me safe, it's trying to block memories and blocking everything else, I know this will pass.

My dad passed away during my breakdown, I attended his funeral still not speaking to my toxic sister and having hardly anyone speak to me after the funeral due to mum and sister telling them all how awful I am, they believed them and I walked away from all of them for ever.

Dad's funeral was actually pretty awful, mum and my sister organised it and mum had this crazy idea that all three of us had to walk hand in hand behind the coffin in some sort of fake show of unity, I felt I had no choice but to agree, anyway I was so drugged up on antidepressants I really wasn't able to argue, so on the day of dad's funeral I walked behind the coffin holding hands with my mum, who was holding hands with my sister, mum was in the middle, luckily because I really wanted to punch that little bitch of a sister, we didn't even look at each other or speak and I haven't touch my mum for years, it was the most weird experience, I didn't cry, I couldn't, I guess it was the meds, I was bloody angry but didn't make a scene, I have better manners and didn't want to prove them right, that I was the awful person they said I was.

Not many people spoke to me because of them and their tales of my awfulness, it's laughable really because anyone who knows me, knows I am not like that at all, never have been, but people are shallow and I'm happy I walked away.
Must mention my bitch of a sister 2 years younger and the golden child, was well known in her village as the local bike , whore in other words, treated her many children by many different men badly and the men even worse, I haven't spoken to her for over 20 years and don't intend to.

My sister stole thousands of pounds from mums bank account after dads death, on the pretence of helping her, myself and my daughter managed to get the bank to pay it back to mum, but my sister still remains to this day the favourite, even though she is currently not speaking to my mum.
My children no longer have anything to do with my mum, their choice, due to mum being nasty towards them and trying to stir trouble, when all they were doing was taking her shopping etc...

Mum currently resides in a Care Home , she faked her way into by pretending to be disabled, the other residents and staff have her sussed out and she's trying to get the council to give her another bungalow because she hates it there, honestly it's true. I've skipped back to this chapter again after a few days break from it, anyone who has experienced trauma will understand how hard it is to revisit experiences that trigger everything from panic attacks to nightmares.

I still feel I am writing this in a way not to upset anyone, which is my people pleasing self coming out, I can't help it, I am constantly people pleasing hoping I might feel valued, wanted, loved, hell I don't feel any of those things even now I have trouble believing anyone even likes me, I hate me so why would anyone like me, I'm damaged goods, dirty, good for nothing, stupid, not good enough.

I hope you are not confused reading this, I have good days, positive days when I do love myself, only recently started to learn this but as I'm writing it will depend on how I'm feeling on the day, this is normal for me.

Baths, I spent hours in the bath from when I was a teenager, guess I was trying to get clean, also it was the only private room in the house, with a towel pushed under the door to keep it shut, mum couldn't get to me.

I also failed to mention the miscarriage I had when I was 17, it was an early miscarriage , I had not had a pregnancy test but was busting out of my clothes and drinking Coke by the pint, one evening I was in the pub with friends and suddenly felt enormous pain in my stomach, went to the toilet and blood was pouring out of me, no mobile phones in those days so had to wait for someone to come and find me, boyfriend at the time was 25, he came to find me, we managed to walk home which wasn't far, with my coat tide around my waist because the blood was now seeping through my jeans right down to my knees, I got home and had to get mum to phone a doctor, she was furious as the doctor saw me alone, and we made up a story about a burst cyst on of ovary, mum didn't believe this for a minute.

The doctor called an ambulance and I was taken to hospital for a couple of days, this was even worse than being at home, I was put in a small ward with 3 other women who were having their tubes tied, they had had their families, I was the youngest one on the ward and although it was stated no children allowed to visit, the woman opposite got permission for her son and family to visit with baby, it really hit me hard seeing the baby, I had them close my curtains around my bed, I was so upset,

I would have kept my baby, I don't believe in abortions anyway. Had a D and C operation and was released home with instructions to rest, no chance I was sent straight out to look for a job, as I was unemployed at the time, I was still very sore and unwell but not allowed to rest or grieve properly, no wonder I'm so fucked up.

Had to go back to the hospital for a scan to check all was clear, the lovely people at the NHS thought it would be fine for me to go and queue up for a scan with all the excited mothers to be, what planet are they on at the NHS, it was a most distressing afternoon, I'm starting to sound like someone in a Victorian novel, most distressing afternoon is an understatement, it was bloody awful, beyond upset, I know 17 probably wasn't a good age to have a baby but I wanted him or her, she would have been mine.

I don't know how I would have coped, I'm sure my boyfriend would have stood by me but I was so very young, a young 17 already broken by life .

Mum was convinced I was having sex every time I left the house and even after spending an afternoon trying to fix my boyfriend's nan's TV set and keep her company, mum attacked me violently when I arrived home, hitting me around the head for being late for tea, I was 18 at that time and was running an accounts department for a local business, I got the job with no maths exams but I looked good in a pencil skirt and the boss liked making me walk up the stairs first, still wasn't good enough for mum.

Mum wasn't all wrong, I was having sex, I had been sexualised by her and the man who abused me at 14, this had a massive impact on me, I developed into a woman who believed sex means love, although I still have trouble believing anyone can really love me, why would they, I don't even love myself. Even though she put me through hell, I still tried on occasions to make some sort of relationship with my mum, you know how people say, "she is still your mum", and I would feel guilty for not having much to do with her, but every attempt ended badly, it might start out well as mum would be pleased to have me around to bitch at but would descend into the same unhealthy nassisstic relationship we always had.

One episode happened when I ended up between houses for 3 weeks, waiting on paperwork to move into a house in the next street to my mum and dad, I asked if I could stay with my 2 children just until the paperwork was completed, it was a straight no, she totally refused and I had to stay in a homeless hostel for 3 weeks until I could move in the house in the next street, it was pretty grim, one room, shared kitchen and bathroom, nowhere near where I was moving too, the people there were very kind to me and couldn't understand why my family let me end up there, even my dad didn't go against my mum and let me stay, he was extremely guilty when he came to the hostel to help me move out.

My sister however moved back in with mum and dad about 6 months later with her 2 children and stayed for about a year, says it all really .

I must mention a breakdown does not come out of nowhere, there are little clues in the lead up to a total mental breakdown, for me it was forgetting simple things, which I would not normally forget, where is my car parked in a row of four or five cars was the first thing I remember being confused about, and then thinking I must be tired, then simple things started to confuse me, it was like my brain could not cope, I was feeling exhausted just trying to get through the day, then I started speaking really slowly it didn't sound like me, I was sent home from work at that point, while trying to convince them I was fine and didn't need to go home, I remember saying my voice sounds different.

 It was down hill all the way, I felt totally numb, self harming, suicidal thoughts just feeling like I couldn't go on, didn't want to go on, needed to stop the pain of my past.

I added this bit about how it feels to start having a breakdown because I'm feeling it again, the little clues are there, I'm forgetting to meet with friends, forgetting to do basic things I wouldn't usually forget and generally feeling down, ok a bit worse than feeling down, feeling like I need drugs, evenings are the worst, I'm currently on 9 coffees a night, I'm thinking they are helping, really need drugs, legal or illegal, I need to be numb again, it's hard to feel feelings which have been hidden for years, I take Night Nurse so I can sleep, I do not recommend this but it is the only way I can get some rest, it's not something I do often.

I will not go back to drugs, I'm strong enough to get through this with coffee and loud music, well if it doesn't work there will be an extra chapter at the end.

Also there was therapy, I tried counselling a few times, that's an understatement I've had 8 counsellors before and after I gave my statement to the police but always walked out after two sessions I couldn't handle talking about my childhood, the last counsellor I saw nearly got me talking I actually went to 4 or 5 sessions with her, but I still wasn't ready to go deeper into my childhood.
Ok I'm getting to the weight loss bit next.

Chapter 4

Rise – State of Nation

The Email that changed my life.

The power of meeting the right person at the right time.

8th July 2016 – Start weight 117.9Kg

Scrolling through Facebook one afternoon, I came across a post in a local group I was in advertising 5 weeks to a healthier you, with pics of women exercising and a offering 2 personal training sessions, and 2 groups Cardio or Spinning , including diet sheet and weight tracking, Zoe McCurdy was the contact and she posted that there were 2 places left for the next 5 week course, starting on the Saturday, very reasonably priced considering I had been looking up gastric band surgery prices.

I've been spending my days walking on the beach collecting Sea Glass and pebbles with holes in them called hang stones, supposed to be lucky and just maybe they are.

So I emailed Zoe stating that basically I was a lost cause, very over weight, had not been exercising for years, getting out of breath walking up our drive which is only a slight slope, I really thought she would message back saying sorry I can't help you.

She messaged back saying I had a place on the course, she sounded nice which was a good start, and invited me to attend a quick meeting on the Saturday evening, OK I'm in but think hell I'm throwing my money away, there is no way I can go to a group and exercise, I don't know anyone and I'm fat and the meeting is at 7pm so I can't have a drink until after, forgot to mention the drink, Vodka and white, or White Wine, as much as it takes to get me drunk, it's taking much more the more I'm getting used to it.

I was smoking but after a chest infection in April I gave up completely, it scared me so much, just went cold Turkey and was fine after a few months, never smoking again.

Saturday came, I'm sitting outside the meeting, scared to go in, I'm wearing Jean's and a baggy top with a cardigan even though it's warm, I try and hide my awful body as much as possible and of course I have a massive handbag to put on my lap to hide my fat stomach behind.
I eventually pluck up the courage to go into the meeting, it's at the local gym, I didn't even know there was a gym there, I do know all the pubs though.
I walk in holding my bag against me trying to hide as much as possible and sit down, Zoe is lovely, she is a professional body builder, who had won medals, I was impressed by her and the fact she has an interest in women's health and fitness.

Zoe is beautiful, with the perfect body, my heart sinks, never in a million years will I ever look that good, I sneak a look at the others in group, I'm pretty sure I'm the fattest in the room.

Some people there had done the previous 5 week challenge and talked about their experiences and to be honest they looked fine to me but they were doing it again to get fitter.

We had to sign up for groups I chose Spinning at 6 30am Monday morning, I know crazy idea but I was hoping not many would go that early, I didn't want to be unable to do it in front of a massive class, I had no intention of doing more that one of each class just once, I don't like groups and the thought of jumping around in tight fitness clothing just embarrassing, that was another thing, where the hell do I get fitness gear to fit me? After a long search Littlewoods Ireland had my size XXL , I bought Nike everything, hoping no one from Nike would see me and sue me for wearing their fitness clothes while fat.

And 7.30pm Cardio Class on a Tuesday, I had no idea what a Cardio class consisted of but realistically didn't think I would attend anyway.

The diet sheet was a different matter, Zoe explained it and I thought yes I could probably do that bit even if I don't do the exercise, so it wouldn't be such a waste of money, I'll get something out of it.

Then my worse nightmare happens, can we all line up for a group photo, OMG, Noooooo, I refuse along with someone else but eventually we both agree and line up for a photo, I'm almost blue breathing in but still looking fat.

Everyone is really friendly, after all we are all here for the same thing, I don't know anyone, it's occurred to me I only know people I meet in the pub, there's loads of people, different people who I've never met before.
Before we go, it gets worse we have to have our measurements taken, I'm dying inside, Zoe is so nice and we have a laugh, she knows it's not easy for me.
I don't know my measurements, I don't want to know.
I buy bathroom scales and kitchen scales and I'm ready to go.

Saturday is weigh in day, first thing in the morning, naked weigh in, send photo of weight to Zoe, every week.

I haven't weighed myself for years and standing in my kitchen naked with my phone trying to take a pic of my weight without the reflection of naked me, it is thankfully a private moment, 117.9K is shocking, lucky II send it to the correct number, I have a fear of messaging my weight to all my contacts.

Diet sheet is printed and I shop for food I can have, which is most things as long as it's the correct weight.
I don't have a sweet tooth, I like savoury food, Taytos , cheese lots of cheese, bread and I'm always hungry especially at night, often get up during the night for a tayto and mayonnaise sandwich with cheese.

I've settled on following the food list, I'm not calling it a diet because it isn't really a diet it's healthy eating, what I should have been doing all along.
I get to eat 4 healthy meals a day no snacking and weigh everything, no problem I think I can manage that and keep a food/exercise diary.

New pens and exercise book and I'm ready to go, it's like first day at school.
I start my new eating regime on the Saturday, after the shock of the weigh in, it's given me a kick in the arse to made the change, little did I know it would change my whole life within a year.

I followed Zoe's advice on preparing food for a few days, mainly because I'm lazy and I wouldn't have to cook everyday and I also have a problem cooking for one, I'm the person who can't judge amounts so would just pour the whole bag of rice in the pot, I must say weighing everything is great, I feel in control of something, I haven't felt in control ever, just kind of falling into things never really in control of anything.

The amount of food is too much I'm eating as much as I can, but 4 meals a day feels a lot, I don't even want a snack I'm not hungry I'm full up.

I've given up drinking due to the calories, so now I'm sobering up I can't sleep, I gave up smoking 3 months ago because of a chest infection, and I've given up sugar, might as well just give everything up, as Eminem says "you've got one shot".

Sports wear is an issue due to my size 24/26, thankfully Littlewoods saved the day and I have Nike leggings and T shirts, if anyone from Nike sees me wearing their kit I'm pretty sure they would take me to court to stop me bringing the brand down.

I feel very exposed in leggings and a t shirt, I never wear short sleeves due to psoriasis cased by stress of sexual harassment from a work colleague a few years ago, he wouldn't leave me alone, even looked in school office diary which had my doctors appointment written in and booked himself a blood test at his doctor on the same day, came back telling staff we were trying for a baby, he was married we were not even friends out of work, it got worse until during student breakfast club he was helping out, he put his arm around me and called me his bitch in front of a room full of students and lucky for me the deputy head teacher, she called me into her office and asked how long it had been going on, and was I ok, he got sacked in the end, but he tried to turn the staff against me first, I know I'm starting to sound like a professional victim but that's how my life has been, most people that know wouldn't even know as I don't discuss it.

Got slightly caught up in that but the thing with writing about my story, it's brings up stuff at odd moments, so I'm just putting them in as they come up, it's a bit like therapy but without the counsellor in a purple dress with her head on one side looking caring, why do they always wear a sensible purple dress and thick red tights? I've got level 3 counselling certificate haven't ever worn a purple dress yet.

My first class is Spinning at 6.30am, no one told me trying to force my 38DDs into a sports bra at 5.30am was going to be so difficult, I'm actually tangled up and stuck in the most weird position like some sort of bondage game, so glad no one can see me.

I'm hoping not many will be up that early, there's 6 of us some I recognise from the meeting others just come to classes, there's a friendly face anyway, one of my WhatsApp buddies is there, Zoe has given us WhatsApp buddies so we can support each other, there are 3 in my group, we've called ourselves the 3 musketeers, the other 2 don't look like they need much exercise, they look great already, we send inspirational memes to keep us going.

Brilliant Zoe has a big speaker and fantastic play list, I have water and a towel, I choose the bike nearest the door incase so I can get out quick if I don't like it, nowhere near enough water for the level of hell that first class was, my legs are on fire, I've never sweated so much in my life, I'm hoping that's a few Kilos gone in sweat, big decision do I drink or breathe, this is 45 minutes of hell I'm dying my legs are like jelly and I can't stand up and peddle, and I'm trying not to get a panic attack, I can't breathe I'm so hot I'm fighting the panic, I think I'm suffocating, I push through, I don't know how but I finished the class, the cool down at the end is my favourite part and Jump Around that song is completely stuck in my head now love it, oh and those photos in magazines of women looking sexy while exercising, it's a lie, my mascara was running down my face in minutes and the faces I pulled were not on the sexy scale, more like death throe of a stranded whale, noises were definitely similar.

Everyone was really friendly, we are all in it together, I did feel a bit better about classes now I know everyone is so nice and no one is judging anyone.

I'm in my car after class, air conditioning on full, thinking it's giving me more Oxygen and wondering how the hell I'm going to use the pedals, how much sweat, I'm soaking, I do hope this sweat weighs something so I will get loss at this weeks weigh in, I get home and really need hoist to get me up the steps into the wagon, I go up sideways and lay down, what the hell have I signed up for.

I did it I have just completed my first class, I feel kind of good I didn't give up, it's a bit of a delayed reaction, I'm very hard on myself and hate myself most of the time but weirdly feeling a little bit good, I'm still fat though, I'm going to have to go to the HIIT class and PT, yes I know one class wasn't going to fix me but I did hope it would.
Realising now why I get to have so much food, I need it to keep going.

I'm going to have to add this reality check, I am so good at faking normal and being positive when I'm not, I have managed to sugar coat that first class, that's the reality of living through trauma, you kind of end up a bit fake, I don't talk about this to anyone so I'm still covering it up, until I read it again, OK the first class was hell, as we started Spinning our bikes, I felt really hot, sweat was pouring from my face actually dripping onto the floor, I was out of breathe and feeling out of control with my breathing, I kept going although I thought I was going into panic, it was the hardest thing I've done my whole body is screaming stop this hurts and my mind was screaming stop you can't breathe you are going to suffocate, but I kept going and kept going fighting every minute of that 45 minute class, it was so hard, but something in me was stirring a strength didn't know I had, while smiling I'm fine to Zoe so she wouldn't get concerned.

And how the hell am I supposed to get a sweat soaked sports bra off?

Tempted to cut it off but can't afford to do that after every class so let the battle commence, I think I lose a bit more weight during the battle of the bra, I win the blasted thing is off, until the next time

PT or Personal Training , sounds like something celebrities have, not someone like me, it comes with it's own issues, I didn't mention it to Zoe but I don't like being touched or being close to people, the whole thing about personal training is that you are close and the trainer is going to have to guide you at times, I figured that I could fake normal for 30 minutes after all Zoe does not know me, I put foundation on my arms again while wearing a t-shirt to cover the Psoriasis and also self harm scars, from a recent meltdown where I used a kitchen knife to cut my right arm after a heavy drinking session, no one told me I would bleed more after alcohol, I had to clean up with a tea towel it was so much blood, this was before I signed up for this challenge but the scars are still there.

I was so nervous, Zoe explained how the session worked, and that weight training would help tighten everything up as I'm losing weight and so would avoid the dreaded sagging, we started, I have never been so embarrassed in my life, it was far worse than Spinning where I was in a group, Zoe was watching every move and I hated it, the exercises were all new to me and between trying to breathe and hoping I wouldn't fart it was hard work, Zoe was great she really put me at ease and had a chat about our families and work, she pushed my lazy self further than I would have ever gone, hell I was even attempting squat jumps which I had not even heard of and I did feel a sense of achievement at the end and a lot of aches, muscles I haven't ever used are being woken up and it hurts, I totally trust Zoe, this is unusual as I have a deep hatred for women all women, I rarely have women as friends and if I do they don't always last long, this I put down to my mother issues and the fact I am a woman and I hate myself.

Zoe believes in me I actually believe that, she has a vibe that connected with me somehow and it's filtering into me and I'm starting to believe in me for the first time.

Decided to bite the bullet and take a full length photo of myself in my workout clothes, there are very few full length photos of me, I usually hide behind a large bag or table, my Facebook photos are all head shots, I take the photo planning to take one at the end of 5 weeks to see if a miracle has occurred and I do look slimmer.

I was never fat even when I had my children always popped back to size 10 no bother, until I had my last child a son, home birth 10lbs no pain relief and two very worried midwives also I knew my marriage was over at that stage, he cooked a Sunday lunch and didn't bring me any, I had to rely on my other children bringing me chocolate and snack food, I was alone that first night and in so much pain like I was giving birth all over again, the pain was so bad I couldn't reach my painkillers in my bedside table, my son was sleeping next to me in a double bed so he was fine and I was breastfeeding so no problem there, I called for help but I wasn't heard had to go through it on my own, there was worse to come, my husband had to leave for a course 6 weeks after the birth, this is the time you can usually have sex again after a normal birth.

I wasn't ready after such a traumatic birth, so he raped on the bedroom floor while my son slept in the bed, finishing with that proves your mine, no I didn't report it and never have.

Yes I've wanted revenge and had a whole load of anger inside me but I'm at peace with myself now at the time of writing, none of this was my fault I'm not a bad person in fact I'm often over nice which annoys me sometimes, I'm not a survivor, I hate that term, I don't know how I see myself, probably confused as I'm still learning who I really am, I've spent years living in survival mode, always felt envious of women who could just be themselves, go out and enjoy themselves, have friends, smile and laugh because they are happy in themselves, I had no idea what that would feel like as I had never felt that way.

First HIIT class, I'm thinking it can't get any worse, but of course it does, here's me who can't walk up our slight uphill drive without getting out of breathe, my partner is always saying why are you out of breathe, anyway I'm at the class not even knowing what a HIIT class is, wishing I had googled it, there's about 12 or so of us and both my WhatsApp buddies are there, it's great to meet them again and have a chat before class, they are both really lovely and very supportive.

HIIT High Intensity Training involves going around the room doing a selection of different exercises which are timed, cardio, core etc...

I'm struggling and sweating like mad, I am trying but it's so hard and I'm so heavy, 117k doing squat jumps isn't easy, I haven't any strength in my arms so every thing is hard, I can't get up from the floor, I have to crawl to the nearest wall and walk up it with my hands to stand up, I really am that unfit, I am also the only one floundering around on the floor like a beached whale.

At least the music is drowning out my heavy breathing and weird grunting, I complete the class and we all say well done to each other, I'm aching like hell, every muscle hurts even muscles I didn't know I had.

I buy protein powder from Zoe, it might help, how I'm not sure but apparently it does, Vanilla flavour, a scoop in my morning porridge is lovely, I felt such a fraud getting this big tub of protein powder out of my car, I'm not a real sports woman, I can only just get through a class in one piece.

1st week done 2 classes and one PT, I don't feel any thinner, I'm still fat but have stuck to the food list, also given up sugar which I loved, and alcohol which I also loved, I haven't slept very well this week due to the lack of alcohol, looking forward to the first weigh in.

Saturday morning 6am standing naked in my kitchen, curtains closed so as not to shock the neighbours, I'm scared to do this incase nothing has changed , phone camera ready, this more complicated than it sounds, get on scales read weight, get off scales, grab phone, take a pic before weight disappears, I'm pleasantly surprised, I have actually lost 1kg, it's not showing anywhere yet but it's gone from somewhere.

I send weight to Zoe, massive congratulations is sent back, I feel really good, this is working.

I have a long way to go but I do feel more positive about losing more, I will stick to the food list and workouts, I am no longer comfort eating, instead I am treating myself with lovely shower gels, mud masks, nail varnish, books, flowers, anything which isn't food and it feels good to really treat myself, mostly it's once a week but sometimes I give myself extra treats if it's been a difficult week emotionally.

Let's get real for a minute, I'm still skipping the hard bits because they are difficult for me to write about, I don't want this to be a lovely I lost weight so can you book, I'm no longer on anti depressants, no longer have alcohol or cigarettes as a crutch, no way of keeping my feelings numb, so I have started to feel feelings that have been hidden for years.

I'm starting to panic walking home from the pub in the dark with my partner, I'm terrified of the dark, have a night light in the bedroom but I'm now feeling like the sky is too low and there's not enough oxygen when it's dark and I'm outside, I'm only drinking coffee at the pub, it's nice to socialize, I have to keep doing breathing exercises, to stop the panic.
We had a power cut one night lol one night, they are actually very common here, I ran out into the garden at night trying to get air, I couldn't breathe, this all steams from my near strangulation years ago, the fear of not being able to breathe doesn't go away.

This is the first time since I was 14 years old, that I've been without anything to numb the pain of a traumatic childhood, even at 14 mum would buy me 6 cans of larger a week on a Friday when she went shopping, not sure why she thought this was ok, but knowing how she liked to be in total control maybe in her mad mind it was a way of keeping me at home.

I didn't smoke until I was 18, I was that terrified of my mum I couldn't chance her finding out, even though one of her friends offered me a cigarette at 15 I didn't take it, knowing it was a trap set by my mum.
Mum was extremely violent and although there were calm times, they didn't last, she was like a volcano, bubbling under the surface until she totally lost it, she was physically violent as well as emotionally abusive all my life, I found out later from an aunt that a few of mums female relatives had been very unstable, it was in the blood.

So my panic attacks are getting worse, my mood is very up and down, I don't feel stable at all, not suicidal though which is good, I arrived here with plan B in mind if things didn't work out.

It's all in the mind I have to stay strong I refuse to let my past beat me, I will win, I suddenly feel this is true, I am strong, I will fight this, I will win.

I refuse to let my life be defined by my past, this is where I finally take control.

Chapter 5

Fighting the hardest battle of my life

Eye of The Tiger – Survivor

Something has changed, I have changed, I can't pinpoint the exact moment of when this change occurred but it happened over the course of the 5 week challenge, suddenly I'm feeling different not physically , I still feel fat, well that could be because I still am classed as obese, it's only been 5 weeks and a miracle didn't occur, I'm not suddenly a super model.

But maybe the miracle did occur but it was mentally not physically that it happened, some how during those first five weeks something changed in my mind, the way I think about myself has changed, no longer feeling like a victim, I feel like a survivor, I have found a warrior spirit inside me that must have been dormant for years but has now come out fighting hard.

That is the only way I can try and describe what happened to me, I had to get to know myself all over again, I was a really a different person.

I was happily losing approximately 1k a week following Zoe's food plan, 2 exercise classes and 1 personal training class a week, people were starting to notice, I was getting a lot of compliments on my weightloss.

Along with compliments comes the haters or fake friends as I call them, "here have a chocolate bar", "bag of Taytos", and there was a large effort put into to getting me drinking again, those concerned know who they are and will remain nameless,

It's sad but there will always be people who wish to see you fail, little did they know, they were actually helping me, no way was I going to fail for them to enjoy it.

During this time I began to learn my body's needs, and it was begging for more exercise alongside what I was already doing. I signed up for another 5 week challenge as I didn't feel I could manage without Zoe tracking my weight.

Then I had to think what else could I do in my spare time to exercise, I needed something I could do on my own, I didn't want to have to try and keep up with someone else or even worse a group.

I decided on running, having never run anywhere in my life, I have no idea why I thought that one up, oh it's free that's why and I can do it on my own.

Healing and change is ugly and painful, it's not pretty, it's not how it's shown in magazines and films, it's painful, sweaty and tearful, I really wish films and newspapers would show the reality of healing and change in a woman.

It is brutal and hellish, you will need to find strength from within that you never knew you had.

How the hell I found that strength I don't know, I just know I was suddenly trying to beat my abusers, they took my childhood, they were not taking my whole life, I'm in my 50s I want my life back, I will beat them, I wasn't given the chance to win in court against them but I can win here in my own life, I can win and I will win, failure is not an option, it really isn't, if I fail I will end up hurting myself, I know that, the pain I live with on a daily basis is hurting me too much now, this my end game, I have to win.

If anyone knew this at the time I'm sure mental health would have been involved, but I don't let anyone close enough to find out and I'm 100% brilliant at faking life, I can smile and laugh while dying inside no problem, it's been my life for years, it comes naturally to me.

Running is not going to be easy, although I am losing weight approximately 1 or 2 kilograms a week, I am still very overweight.
I have added long walks in between classes and PT, just feeling that my body wanted more, walking up to 4k on the beach, started at just 2k walks and built it up to include hills, well slight slopes really but anything that causes me to be out of breath is a hill in my book.

So after walking 4k I was getting bored and wasn't feeling challenged enough, besides I like walking it's easy and I can walk like a slug no problem, but my mind and body wanted a challenge do more work harder, so I started to add a tiny little run in with the walk, I don't think it was an actual run, more of me trying to drag my fat legs a little bit faster while trying to breathe for 30 seconds, it was awful, I couldn't breathe properly, I definitely couldn't run, which is why I was on the beach at 6am before anyone was up to see me, but I wanted to beat myself, I wanted to beat all those you will amount to nothing comments from my childhood , so went hard on myself , my self talk wasn't nice, mostly work bitch, do it, just do it, I really hope none heard me.

I tried headphones and music but I feel like I can breathe with headphones on, I don't even breathe out of my ears, but if you've had panic attacks you will know, you don't need anything blocking any part of you, hats were also a no go, had a Bum bag for my car keys which I could wear for about 5 minutes then would have to unclip it and carry it, it made me feel like I was be strangled around my stomach, this was all in my mind.

So I could only run in trainers, socks, running leggings a sports bra and t-shirt, I could tolerate a running hoodie if it was raining.

The more I tired to run the more I would get panic attacks, they made me feel like ripping all my clothes of there and then, everything felt right.
At first I would stop and drive home crying with the air conditioning on in the car so I could breathe, but then I got totally bloody minded and forced myself to go on by stopping turning around and going at a walk until breathing returns to normal then running again.

This took a lot of working on but I ended up getting less and less panic and more running.
I started to work on distance, started jogging 1k, the next day I jogged 1.30k by the next weekend I was jogging 2k on the running machine and then with my trainer jogged around the Hurling pitch twice, I went home after that was me totally done for the day, going outside was stressful but pleased I did it.

On the running machine I could see my reflection in the window, used to pretend I was Rocky Balboa, not that I look anything like him, but the running scene from one of his films and Rocky never gives up.
Being outside with my trainer was very difficult, I was so used to being on my own or on a running machine I was terrified of jogging with her, would I be able to keep up or even keep going, thought I was going to fail.
I did it, I really did it, that was one hell of an achievement for me.

I found running outdoors really difficult, just the thought of being seen running made me anxious, I know no one would really take any notice of a fat woman trying to run but in my head the whole world is laughing and wanting me to fail. The running machine is my comfort zone, I feel safe and love tracking my distance and time, although I am very slow, it hardly counts as running, the fitness tracker on my phone does not recognise it as a run, I obviously running at slug speed.

I'm calling it running because I'm out of breathe, sweating and moving slightly faster than a walk so for me it's a run. Zoe suggests that I sign up for a local 4k road race in November, it's September so plenty of time to train for it and I would have a target and recorded finish time, Zoe will run with me at my pace.

I agree and instantly regret it, how the hell am I going to pull this off, a 4k race, people will be there for a start, I can't imagine running with other people, plus they will be actual runners, really fit people, I am a heap of nerves about it, I have 6 weeks to train for this, why the hell I agreed I don't know.

Chapter 6

Inspired by Race Horses

Champions Theme from the film Champions, the Bob Champion Story

I finished writing this book on the 40th Anniversary of Aldaniti's Grand National win.

This is where I get weird, I love horses and horse racing, one of my daughters is named after a Jennie Pitman trained horse, unfortunately she doesn't like horses as much as I do.
I started think about Red Rum, he won 3 English Grand Nationals, he was often trained on the beach, here's me comparing myself to a Thorough Bred when I'm more Shetland Pony with a serious weight problem.

And Aldaniti came back from injury to win the Grand National along with Jockey Bob Champion who beat cancer, while Aldaniti was healing, together they proved anything is possible.

I begin to train myself the same way they train racehorses, it might seem strange but it worked, horses that are hyped up at the start and refuse to go into the stalls are walked around in a circle to calm down, then 's they go in, I started to do this every time a panic attack started during running.

Walk in a circle and if I could start running again in a different direction, if not just run again in the same direction when calm and go at a slower pace, reminding myself I can breathe, I will not suffocate.

This technique really worked for me, I no longer needed to stop and go home, I could manage my breathing during the run.

The beach is great for race horses legs, so I stay on the beach for my training, I am actually scared to go anywhere near a road or hard ground incase my knees give up, having never run, I don't know what my legs can cope with, so I'm taking it easy on the soft sand.
Some people find it harder to run on the beach but I love it, the sea, the sunrise, the wind and rain, I love it all, especially if there is no one there.

Unfortunately my running technique needs a lot of work, I run like a rabid zombie, it's definitely not graceful like a race horse. I have to run with my mouth open to breathe and mostly have my tongue out as well, nose running and foaming at the mouth along with the weird legs close together gait, because I'm scared of wetting myself, thank goodness for Tena Lady, if anyone saw my adjusting my pants while running it was because things move and I don't want to look like I have a Mickey (Dick).

Racehorses also swim in the sea, I would love to swim in the sea, but no way can I even think of wearing a swimming costume in public, I know no one would probably notice but in my warped mind I just think everyone would be looking at how fat I am.

Visualization has been a great help, visualise running further, loving the adrenaline rush of completing what I set out to do, however small the target.

I also do a racing commentary during my run, I do this in my head as much as possible but pretty sure I forget and start doing it out loud, "She's off, the going is soft to wet, slow to start but she's gaining ground now, she's lengthened her stride and is going for the finish line", crazy as it sounds it works for me.

I work myself hard, if for some reason I don't make a target, I would be out first thing the next morning and make myself hit the target after a night of beating myself up mentally for not being good enough.

Sometimes I am physically sick while running, I just start again after, I will not give up.

I start practising lengthening my stride so I can stop running like I'm trying not to wet myself, weirdly I'm not anymore, I guess with losing weight I'm more in control of my bladder during exercise.
I also change my lead leg occasionally, yes I know I only have 2 legs but I usually lead with my left leg, changing it gives it a break especially if I feel an ache in it.

Breathing is still a massive issue, I have a pocket full of tick tacs for every run, sucking on a tick tac at least keeps my mouth shut for awhile and takes my mind off breathing only for a short time, then I'm back to running like a fish out of water, gasping for air, but I'm working on it, I'm determined this is not going to beat me.

I eventually get the 4k, yes I'm slower than a snail though peanut butter, but I can get the distance needed for the road race, ok 4k on the beach is not going to be the same as 4k on the road, no idea if my legs will cope with a road run, they have muscles now from running, spinning and weight training in PT so I'm hoping they will hold out.
The major battle is going on in my mind.

I have never felt good enough , even now, I feel a total fake, people are coming up to me after class saying "you look great", "you are doing really well" and worst of all "you inspire me", I can't understand why anyone would be inspired by me, I feel like I'm faking it, they don't know the whole story.

I know I should be thrilled but at this stage I was still dealing with feelings and emotions that had been hidden for so long, I get emotional a lot, I cry after every run and sometimes after a class, I still can't believe I'm doing this, really doing this.
Everyone is so kind to me, I really am not used to it and really don't think I deserve it, they only see me as turning up to class working hard and losing weight.

They have no idea of the battle I am fighting inside my head, I don't want to heal, I don't want to feel feelings, I am weirdly content detached from these things.

With transformation comes healing weather you want it or not, I was definitely not ready for this and given the option would have walked away in the same way I had walked out of every therapy session I have ever tried when it looked like things were going to go deep, I was out of the door and home before I could get hurt again.

Well that was logical to my survival, I have never really wanted to heal, to heal you need to feel the pain again, acknowledge it and release it, let it go, I prefer to block everything painful, I don't want to deal with painful memories when it's easier to block them and just fake happiness.

Over the years I have had a fantastic work record, I always have been the one anyone can talk to, strangers at the bus stop would feel able to tell me their private problems, even abuse they have never talked about before, maybe people can feel my energy and know I understand, I would always listen and direct them to the correct services.

I seemed to help everyone but me, I have no interest in helping myself, I feel like I don't deserve help, I'm not worth anything. But slowly things are shifting in my head, there are so very bad days, feelings coming up to the surface, on these days, I can't function, I can't exercise, I sleep, mainly because that is my go to coping process, I can't feel anything while sleeping, unless nightmares come, I curl up under a quilt and sleep for hours and hours, between bouts of crying uncontrollably.
I want to hurt myself but I don't, I message Zoe and explain the situation, feeling like a failure, she totally understands and her wise words really help get thing in perspective .

I have rest days, I usually walk on the beach and paddle in the sea, even if it's cold, it's good for my feet. I start to spend more time on the beach trying to run as far as I can, I have no idea what my body is capable of so every time I get comfortable with a distance I tag another 1k on the end, loving the feeling I get when I reach another target.

Also beginning to understand my body and it's needs, I think I've spent my life avoiding my feelings and numbing them, only now have I started to hear my body, I can feel when I need a longer run or another HIIT class, I started to do 2 classes a week, plus Spinning and PT, my body wanted more, I could actually feel it wanting more.

The same went for food as I upped my exercise I eat to feed for the exercise so altered my food intake accordingly, I have no experience of nutrition only what I have learned from Zoe and by listening to my body, just went with what I felt I needed, funny my body never needed cakes, chocolate or things like that, I don't miss or want any of it.

I am not feeding my emotions with food anymore as I'm sticking to the 4 meals a day and besides although I enjoy my meals, I see them as fuel, if it's not going to fuel me, I'm not eating it.
Totally transforming my life wasn't something I thought would happen, after all I only signed up to lose weight.
It's all so new, I'm realising now how much I've blocked my feelings, no wonder I come across as a hard bitch at times, not intentionally just to protect myself.

During this time Zoe has been to France and became A World Champion Body Builder, which is so fantastic, so proud of her, she is such an incredible woman and an inspiration.

Chapter 7

Race Day and Beyond

Unstoppable – Sia

Current Weight - 100kg.7g

The last words from Zoe last night were, "get a good nights sleep", no chance of that, my anxiety is through the roof, I am going to have to run this 4k road race, everyone at the exercise classes know I am doing it, I didn't mind Zoe telling the other members of the group about it, everyone is so very kind, wishing me luck and, some ladies tell me how I am an inspiration to them, I feel so honoured that I am inspiring other women and I hope by finishing this 4k it will inspire more women to gain the confidence to join us at the exercise groups, if I can do this, anyone can.

At least it's only the people from the group who know I'm doing this, I still haven't told anyone I know what I am doing, yes people have noticed my weight loss and have had some lovely comments, but there's always one who wants to watch me fail, offering chocolate etc..

I tell them I've joined the gym, they don't need to know anything else, I'm very private at the best of times, hate sharing information that could be used against me at a later date, I know that's a little paranoid but it's been proven time and time again by my mother and others.
I get up at 6am and have my usual breakfast of porridge, everything must be the same as a training run, I am so emotional, crying and crying, I really can't believe I'm doing this.

I feel I am doing this not just for me but for every abused girl and woman out there who has not found their strength to begin their own healing journey , I know in my heart I will tell my story one day.

I keep jumping from excited to scared, to upset, I have good luck messages on our WhatsApp group chat from the other women in my exercise groups, that is so lovely and means so much when they say they are inspired by me, makes me cry even more.

I can't turn up for my first race looking like I've been crying all night, ok headphones on and some loud music, that will definitely help.

It's a cold November morning, it's dry so that's a bonus, I'm on my period which is a worry, due to the Menopause I have been having the most awful heavy painful periods, going to have to run with a thick sanitary towel on and fingers crossed I don't leak.

I drive to the race venue, I know where the start is, I have looked at the route online an aerial view, didn't get the chance to run it before hand, so I don't really know the route, everything looks different from above and I don't know the area anyway.
I meet Zoe, I feel better immediately , she calms me down and we head to register, my first shock is the amount of runners, real fit runners, I am thinking I am definitely in the wrong place, what the hell am I thinking, everyone looks so fit and me I am still fat, I feel like I am sticking out like a sore thumb.
We warm up with a light jog to the start line, we aim for the very back of the pack, it's way back from the start line, it's also a fairly narrow lane to start before we get on to the road.
I feel very claustrophobic there are so many runners, I can't even see the start, everyone is very friendly.

Zoe is going to run at my snail like pace so no pressure there, but OMG I'm running with a World Champion bodybuilder, what if I can't do this?

The waiting is the worst thing, I'm trying to focus and tell myself I can run this distance , it's mostly flat and there's no reason I can't finish this 4k race.
Unfortunately my fears are over taking and I'm thinking what if I fail? What if I can't do this?
I am so scared I will fail.
I need to do this for me, I need to beat my fears and prove I am good enough, I will not be beaten by my past.
Suddenly everyone goes quiet, OMG this it, I can't get out of it now.

There's a loud blast from a air horn and we are off.
My legs instantly turn to jelly and I can't breathe, shit I'm in trouble already and I haven't even crossed the start line yet.
it is quite a slow start thankfully, the lane is so narrow and there are so many runners it seems a long time before we actually reach the start line, other runners are already passing us, that's fine, I am not racing anyone, I am running my own race, it's me against my demons.

As we turn out into the road I am shocked to see it lined with people clapping, I feel sick, my breathing isn't good I am struggling with panic.

I hear my name shouted out from the crowd by more than one person, wow I have so much support , it really helps, I can give up now.
Worse to come I have to run past the camera filming the start, doing my best to try and look normal, I hold my breathe and keep my mouth shut, and wipe my nose on my jacket, that doesn't help matters but at least I look kind of normal.

The whole pack of runners has pounded off ahead, I can see their heads bobbing along in the distance, I'm thankful we are finally on our own.

Breathing not settled, nose running and I am dribbling when we pass my friend who is recording the moment on video, I can't wipe my nose on my sleeve now so I just hope it can't be seen from that distance, wipe nose on sleeve as soon as we have passed her, thinking it's safe but unfortunately she was still filming and there's me wiping away madly with my sleeve.

I manage to keep the same pace for the whole race, never really settled and my breathing was awful the whole way. But Zoe kept me going with high fives and thumbs up, I just kept plodding onwards, with no idea where I was and more importantly where the finish was.

I struggle through, my throat is sore from breathing in the cold air and then finally I can see the finish line, I am so relieved, I can't believe I have done this, Zoe grabs my hand and holds it up like a champion and we run together to the finish line, I can't breathe, I'm shaking and crying, someone throws me a race t-shirt and my friends from class are there to congratulate me, one gives me a bottle of water, I am so thankful for that water, although should I breathe or drink, I can't do both. Everyone was so lovely, I felt like I had just run a marathon, so many people congratulated me and my phone had messages popping up for the rest of the day.

I wasn't even last, nearly but not quite, time was 36 minutes.

I drive home crying all the way, this wasn't just a 4k race it was far more than that, I really feel like I am beating my demons.

Something has really changed in me, just finishing that race was the first time I have ever felt good enough for just being me. I have a long way to go but I will not give up, I am starting to like myself a little, I had no idea that day what I would achieve in the next year.

Chapter 8

Just Me

Current Weight - 60kg

Total Weight Loss – 48.9kg in 18 months and I have abs to be proud of.

Bon Jovi – It's My Life

Wow it's unreal how much life changes when you lose a massive amount of weight, suddenly everyone is talking to me, giving me compliments and asking how I lost so much weight and saying how great I am looking.

At the end of the day it was my trauma which was the problem, once that was starting to heal so my weight problem was sorted, and the exercise kick started the whole process, I have probably been told this many times and read it in self help books over the years but honestly until I was really near rock bottom I could never understand it or believe it.
This is all lovely but as a very quiet, private person I did find it hard to handle all the attention every time I went out, this must be how Celebrities feel.

Sometimes I just feel like hiding from the World, I am nothing special, I've done nothing special, I am just me.

But who the hell am I?

That's what I have to find out, I am slowly getting to know the real me, the me that has always been hidden and trodden down by years of abuse.

And I am beginning to love myself, I don't hate me any more and I definitely don't want to destroy myself in anyway, I realise now it wasn't me I was trying to destroy, it was feelings, memories all the stuff that hurts me, I just wanted to be free of the pain. It hasn't been an easy journey, I am still learning how to really feel feelings, good and bad, I've spent so long numbing feelings I have no idea what they feel like and how to deal with them. To be honest I don't like it, feelings can be difficult and they are coming at unexpected times causing me to crash mentally for days at a time, I am tempted to numb them again with meds or alcohol but I am staying strong, my need to run and be fit is overriding my need for meds and alcohol.

Since that first 4k race I did 3 more of the same race, each race a month apart and each race I finished faster than the previous one, knocking minutes off my time, ok I was still not very fast but I could see improvement.

After that was a 5k Park Run which went well due to not knowing where the start was, we were all called to follow someone with a flag to the start and suddenly we were off, no time to panic just run, it was a twice around a park route so a nice run, kept my pace and finished in 40 minutes.
I also increased weight training with Zoe to 3 sessions a week and 2 HIIT classes.

A bit of a love hate relationship with weight training, which is why I upped it to 3 sessions a week, it's definitely a challenge for me, but that just makes me work harder, results are good, my body is changing shape and getting more muscular and it's also helped stop any major skin sagging along with just luck. Fast forward 18 months and I am now running 10 miles along the coast road every Saturday, love a few hills, enjoying challenging myself, 16 miles is my max at the moment.

I am definitely a long distance runner at my happiest running for hours on my own, this book was written in my head on my long runs.

Lost a couple of toe nails and finally feel like a real runner. Training changes month to month, changing from my favourite long distance runs to a month of 5k and 4k fast runs to build up my speed, which is getting there.
I'm totally happy with those results, continuing to chip away at these times so will be running faster by the time you read this. After 30 years I have finally back in the saddle, as soon as I reached my riding weight of 70k I booked my first riding lesson in 30 years.

I have always had a love of horses and this was a big dream of mine to lose enough weight to ride again, I'm crying typing this it was so emotional to be riding a horse again, and although very rusty, I wasn't too bad first time out, currently learning to jump which I love, I am total adrenaline junkie.

I started swimming in the sea in the summer , wearing a swimming costume and shorts, sometimes just a sports bra and my sports leggings if I couldn't be bothered getting changed, bought a waterproof car seat cover so it was fine to drive home a little wet.

I swim at least once a week all through winter, wearing a wetsuit and love the freedom of swimming in the sea, no longer embarrassed by my body.
I weigh myself every Saturday morning, my weight has be stable for months now and that's how I will keep it
Due to Covid lockdown races have been stopped but will run a half marathon when we get back to normal.
Have raised money for the Mater Hospital, running 100 miles in a month challenge, I completed the 100 miles in 14 days. Will do more fundraising runs in the future.

I still collect Sea Glass, it reminds me of my healing, being bashed by life but ended up smooth and beautiful. Yeah I feel beautiful sometimes, not always but sometimes I think I look ok.

I'm laughing at that previous sentence, I really have gone soft, that's not a bad thing, I don't feel like life is one big battle ground anymore.

My fight is still there but being put to good use into the running, weight training and horse riding
And lastly there is no way I could have achieved any of this without the total support of my trainer and friend Zoe and Lizette who have been there for me every time I fell apart and believed in me from day one and all the support I received along the way from the lovely members of Zoe's exercise classes, I can't thank you all enough.

My children who had to live with me during some of my worst times have been fantastic with their love and support and constant cups of tea and toast, I couldn't have got through the bad times and coming off meds without them.
And of course a big thank you to my partner who has had to live through this process with me and has provided total love and support all the way, wouldn't be without him, would have liked to have written more about him but he doesn't want to be in the book.

My life now is very different, I have real friends, women friends, now I'm feeling able to let people get close to me, no longer hating women because of my mother issues, doing things I enjoy for myself, putting my needs first, and actually enjoying the ups and downs of life.
I really feel loved just for being me and I no longer feel like I have to save everyone, I am a peace with my past and it is in the past.

My wardrobe is full of lovely dresses, blouses and skinny Jean's, no longer need to cover my body with baggy clothes, I wear clothes that fit and feel confident walking along the street.

I haven't had a panic attack for a while now, possibly because I can manage them better when I feel one coming on, so not getting the full blown panic attack I used to get, I have learned to breathe.

Not getting triggered by news stories and films as much as I did, although I still get nightmares occasionally, I can sleep in a dark room without a night light most nights.
Still not comfort eating, that was all due to the trauma and me not dealing with the feelings, I don't need to feed my feelings now.

Not smoking, drinking or medicated, not that I need medicating now but it came close during the writing of some chapters, I don't ever want to go down those routes again and I know I won't.

These days I am a softer person, not living in survival mode anymore, so not trying to constantly defend myself or fight, happy to get to know people and give them a chance instead of blocking everyone out and even hugged people and allowed people to hug me and I'm fine with that.

Cork is has been my home for a few years now and I love it here, I wouldn't want to be anywhere else on Earth, I believe being here was a big part of my healing, Cork and it's people are very special to me and I will always be thankful for the friendship and support I have here.

I am even learning the Irish language, if you ever pass me while I'm driving, I'm not talking to myself I am repeating Irish words from a CD.

I was going to end the book on "There is no happy ending" but I really think there is happiness, it was inside me all along. Real happiness feels different, it's lighter, no darkness hiding behind it and I'm enjoying that, I don't ever remember feeling real happiness.

And love I can really feel it and give it, it's unconditional. There will still be bad days to get through, but I am well able to handle my feelings good or bad.

And no writing my story didn't kill my demons, I still get moments sometimes when I just sitting calmly with a cup of tea on my own and suddenly my stomach will twinge and drop like when you are on a rollercoaster, for no current reason, then I know it's a panic attack and can get myself grounded before it takes hold, move, go outside or put tv on, count things anything to bring myself back to now.

I have awful trouble relaxing, I can't, I need to be doing something, even at home I wear headphones constantly so I can listen to radio dramas, I can't have silence, memories come back too quickly .
Good peaceful calm days outweigh the bad days, it's very strange having a few good days in a row, I start to think there's something wrong, why am I so calm, I'm just not used to it after years in survival mode, it is really nice to be so calm, the relaxing bit will come in time, I'm still learning.
But mostly I am healed, I feel healed only sometimes I can hear echoes of the past.

I really would love to say I feel good enough but the reality is even after achieving so much in a relatively short space of time, I still do not feel good enough, I guess this may come, healing doesn't happen all at once and maybe not ever, I can live with it either way, it's not the problem it once was.

The biggest thing that triggered my healing was someone believed in me and somewhere deep inside I believed them. The trauma happened, it's not going away just because I've written it down, but it has helped to leave it in the past, I think when I physically put this book into a drawer and close it, that will be the end.

I am not a victim, I am not a survivor, I am just me and that is enough.

I have missed out a lot of traumatic events or the details of events, apart from protecting my own mental health, I don't see that it's healthy for anyone to be reading in depth details of these events.

I really hope my story will give someone hope that, there is a future no matter how bad things are, there can be healing, it's never too late to take your first steps to change your life, but you have to take that first step yourself, go towards what feels right for you, it maybe fitness, it maybe counselling or therapy, or something completely different.
And don't be afraid to tell your story, surround yourself with people you can talk to and trust, if you don't have that now, it will come as you heal and open up more.
I never believed this until it happened to me, I was resigned to being a victim, but healing and change can happen when you least expect it.

Printed in Great Britain
by Amazon

70251198R00045